Back Pai

Exercises for Seniors

Simple Exercises and Stretches to Relief Lower Back Pain, Heal Painful Joints, Improve Mobility and Prevent Injuries.

Shawn West

Table of Contents

Overview Of Back Pain

Back pain is a common condition that affects a significant portion of the population. It is caused by a variety of factors, including injury, poor posture, overuse, and degenerative conditions such as osteoarthritis. The pain can range from a dull ache to a sharp, stabbing sensation and can be accompanied by stiffness and muscle spasms. In some cases, it can also radiate down the legs and cause numbness or tingling. Back pain can be acute (short-term) or chronic (long-term) and can have a significant impact on a person's quality of life, making it difficult to perform daily activities and even work.

The lower back is made up of a complex network of bones, muscles, tendons, and ligaments that work together to support the upper body and allow for movement. The lower back is also subject to a lot of stress and strain due to the constant movement and weight-bearing that it must endure. As a result, it is prone to injury and pain. Common causes of lower back pain include muscle strains, herniated discs, spinal stenosis, and osteoarthritis.

Lower back pain can be treated with a variety of methods, including medication, physical therapy, and surgery. However, exercise is a key component of lower back pain relief, as it can help to strengthen the muscles that support the lower back and improve flexibility and range of motion. Exercise can also improve overall fitness and help to prevent future episodes of pain.

Why Exercise Is Important

Exercise is an important aspect of lower back pain relief, as it can help to improve muscle strength, flexibility, and range of motion. When the muscles that support the lower back are strong and flexible, they are better able to support the spine and take pressure off of the bones and joints. This can help to reduce pain and improve overall function.

Several types of exercise can be beneficial for lower back pain relief, including:

Stretching exercises: Stretching can help to improve flexibility and reduce muscle tension, which can lead to less pain and improved mobility. Hamstring stretches, quad stretches, glute stretches, and lower back stretches can be particularly helpful.

Strengthening exercises: Strengthening the core muscles, including the back, abs, and glutes, can help to improve posture and take pressure off of the lower back. Core exercises such as planks, bridges, and bird dogs can be effective.

Aerobic exercises: Aerobic exercises can help to improve overall fitness and reduce inflammation, which can also help to reduce pain. Brisk walking, cycling, or swimming are good options.

Yoga: Yoga can help to improve flexibility, strength, and balance, as well as reduce stress, which can all contribute to lower back pain relief.

Understanding the lower back

Anatomy and function

The lower back is made up of a complex network of bones, muscles, tendons, and ligaments that work together to support the upper body and allow for movement. The main bones in the lower back include the lumbar vertebrae, which are the five large bones that make up the lower part of the spine. The lumbar vertebrae are connected by intervertebral discs, which act as cushions and allow for movement.

The muscles in the lower back include the erector spinae, which run along the spine and are responsible for maintaining posture and allowing for movement; the quadratus lumborum, which is located on the sides of the spine and helps to maintain stability; and the gluteus maximus, which is the largest muscle in the body and is located in the buttocks. These muscles work together to support the spine and allow for movement.

The tendons and ligaments in the lower back include the supraspinous and interspinous ligaments, which run between the vertebrae and provide stability, and the iliolumbar and sacrotuberous ligaments, which connect the spine to the pelvis.

The lower back plays a crucial role in supporting the upper body and allowing for movement. The muscles, tendons, and ligaments work together to maintain the proper alignment of the spine and allow for movement, such as twisting, bending, and lifting. When any of these structures are damaged, it can lead to lower back pain and limited mobility.

It's important to note that the lower back is also responsible for protecting the spinal cord, which is the bundle of nerves that runs through the spine and controls the movement of the body, thus any injury or damage to the lower back can result in serious consequences.

Common Causes Of Back Pain

There are several common causes of lower back pain, including:

Muscle strains: Overuse or injury to the muscles in the lower back can lead to strains, which can cause pain and stiffness. Strains are often caused by overuse, such as from repetitive motions or heavy lifting, or by sudden movements that put too much stress on the muscles.

Herniated discs: The intervertebral discs in the lower back can become damaged and bulge out, putting pressure on the nerves in the spine and causing pain. This condition is also known as a slipped or ruptured disc.

Spinal stenosis: This condition occurs when the spaces in the spine narrow, putting pressure on the nerves and causing pain. It is often caused by degenerative conditions such as osteoarthritis or spinal degeneration.

Osteoarthritis: This is a degenerative condition that can cause wear and tear on the joints in the lower back, leading to pain and stiffness.

Sciatica: This is a condition where the sciatic nerve, which runs from the lower back to the legs, is compressed or irritated, causing pain that radiates down the leg.

Poor posture: Sitting or standing in a hunched position for prolonged periods can cause the muscles and ligaments in the lower back to become fatigued and lead to pain.

Obesity: Carrying extra weight can put extra stress on the lower back and cause pain.

Stress and Anxiety: High levels of stress and anxiety can cause muscle tension and lead to lower back pain.

These are some of the most common causes of lower back pain, however, back pain can be caused by a variety of other factors, and it's important to consult a healthcare professional to determine the specific cause of your pain.

Warm-up Exercises for Seniors

Warm-up exercises are an important part of any exercise routine, as they help to prepare the body for activity and reduce the risk of injury. For seniors with lower back pain, warm-up exercises can help to loosen up tight muscles, improve flexibility, and increase blood flow to the lower back.

Cat-Cow Stretch

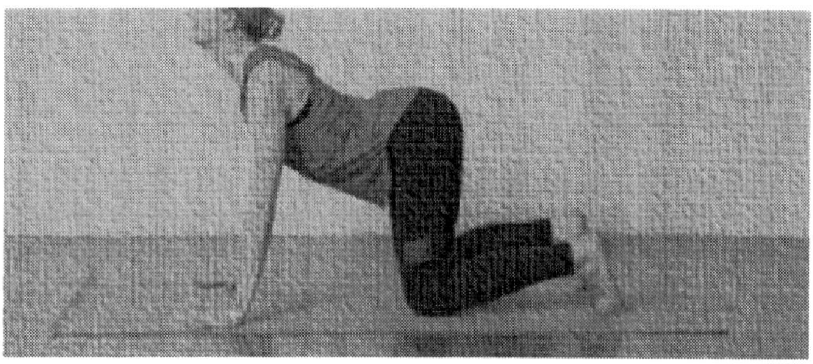

Steps:

- Start on your hands and knees, with your wrists directly under your shoulders and your knees directly under your hips.

- As you inhale, arch your back, lift your head, and bring your tailbone towards the ceiling.

- As you exhale, round your back, tuck your chin to your chest, and bring your tailbone towards your knees.

- Repeat this movement for a few minutes.

Hamstring Stretch

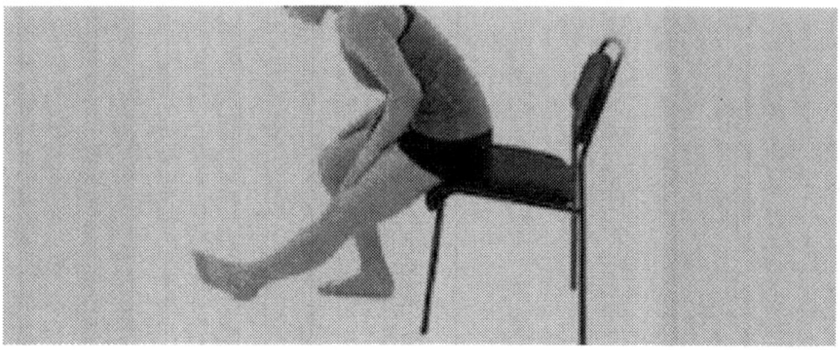

Steps:

- Sit on the edge of a chair or bench with your feet flat on the floor.

- Slowly straighten your right leg, keeping your left foot on the floor.

- Reach forward with both hands and try to touch your toes.

- Hold the stretch for a few seconds and then relax. Repeat the stretch with the other leg.

Shoulder Blade Squeeze

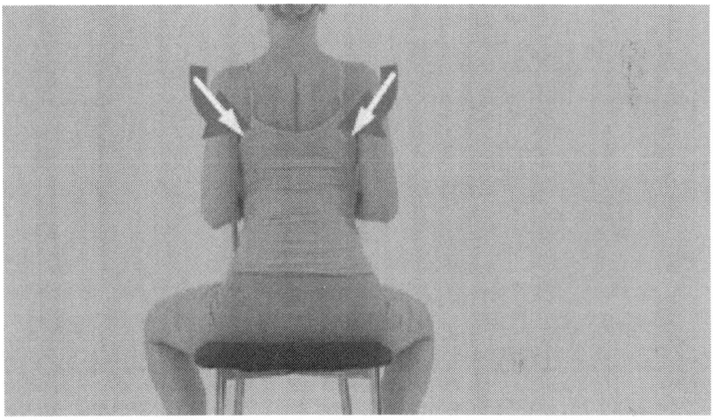

Steps:

- Stand up straight and squeeze your shoulder blades together.

- Hold the squeeze for a few seconds and then relax.

- Repeat the exercise for a few minutes.

Torso Twist

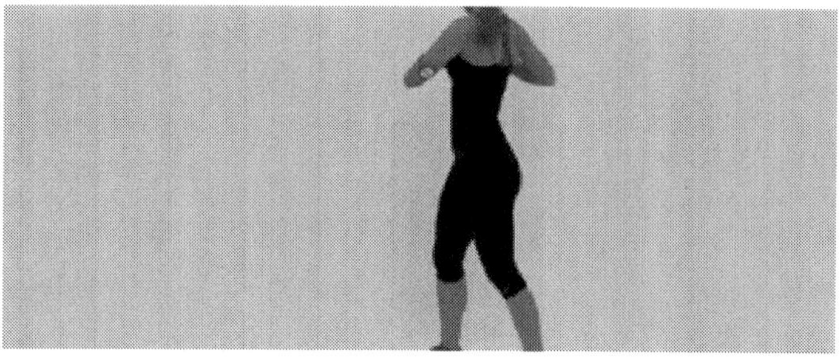

Steps:

- Stand up straight and cross your right arm over your left arm.

- Slowly twist your torso to the left as far as you can without causing pain.

- Hold the stretch for a few seconds and then relax.

- Repeat the exercise on the other side.

Strengthening Exercises

Superman

The Superman exercise is great for seniors to help relieve lower back pain and improve core strength. The exercise is named after the superhero because it mimics the position of Superman flying.

Here's how to perform the Superman exercise:

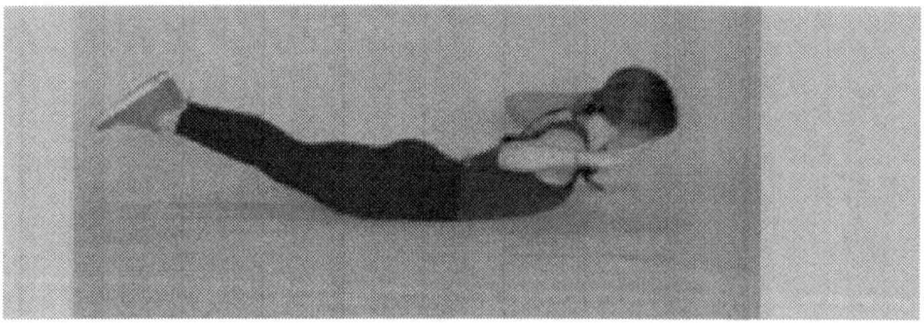

- Lie face down on a mat or soft surface with your arms and legs extended.

- Slowly raise your arms, legs, and chest off the ground as high as you can, keeping your head and neck in line with your spine.

- Hold the position for a few seconds and then lower your arms, legs, and chest back down to the starting position.

- Repeat the exercise for a set number of repetitions, usually 8-12 reps, and 2-3 sets.

This exercise works on the lower back, glutes, and core muscles. It helps to improve your posture and balance.

It's important to start with a small number of repetitions and gradually increase as you become stronger. It's also important to maintain proper form and technique, to avoid injury and achieve the best results.

It's always a good idea to consult with a healthcare professional before starting any exercise program, especially if you have a chronic condition or have had a recent injury. They can also help to adapt the exercise to your individual needs and limitations.

Heel raises

Heel raises are a great exercise for seniors to help relieve lower back pain and improve the strength of the lower leg muscles. The exercise involves lifting the heels off the ground while standing and then lowering them back down.

Here's how to perform the heel raises exercise:

- Stand with your feet hip-width apart and your arms at your sides.

- Slowly raise your heels off the ground as high as you can, keeping your knees straight.

- Hold the position for a few seconds and then lower your heels back down to the starting position.

- Repeat the exercise for a set number of repetitions, usually 8-12 reps, and 2-3 sets.

This exercise works on the calf muscles and the ankle joint. It helps to improve your balance and stability. Heel raises are an easy exercise to do and can be done anywhere, even while standing in a queue.

It's important to start with a small number of repetitions and gradually increase as you become stronger. It's also important to maintain proper form and technique, to avoid injury and achieve the best results.

Knee To Chest Stretch

The knee-to-chest stretch is a great exercise for seniors to help relieve lower back pain and improve flexibility in the back and hips. This stretch is simple and easy to do and can be done in the comfort of your own home.

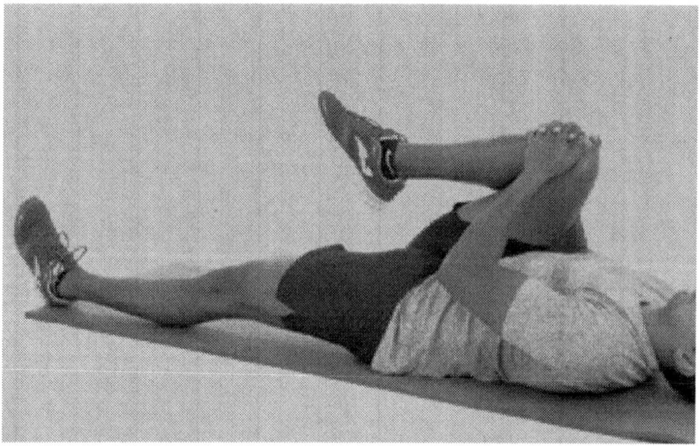

Here's how to perform the knee-to-chest stretch:

- Start by lying on your back with your knees bent and your feet flat on the floor.

- Slowly bring one knee up towards your chest, using your hands to gently pull the knee in.

- Hold the stretch for a few seconds, breathing deeply and feeling the stretch in your lower back.

- Slowly lower your leg back down to the starting position, and repeat the stretch with the other leg.

- Repeat the exercise for a set number of repetitions, usually 8-12 reps, and 2-3 sets.

This exercise is a fantastic way to relieve tension in your lower back and improve flexibility in your hips. It's a gentle way to stretch your muscles and help to keep them supple. This exercise is perfect for seniors who want to improve their mobility and reduce back pain.

It's important to start with a small number of repetitions and gradually increase as you become stronger. Remember to breathe deeply and relax while doing this exercise, and maintain proper form and technique to avoid injury and achieve the best results.

Pelvic Tilt

The pelvic tilt exercise is great for seniors to help relieve lower back pain and improve core strength. The exercise involves tilting the pelvis to engage the abdominal and lower back muscles.

Here's how to perform the pelvic tilt exercise:

- Start by lying on your back with your knees bent and your feet flat on the floor.

- Slowly contract your abdominal muscles and tilt your pelvis upward, pressing your lower back into the floor.

- Hold the position for a few seconds, and then relax your

abdominal muscles and release the tilt.

- Repeat the exercise for a set number of repetitions, usually 8-12 reps, and 2-3 sets.

This exercise works on the abdominal and lower back muscles. It helps to improve your posture and stability. Pelvic tilt exercise is easy to perform and can be done even while lying down.

It's important to start with a small number of repetitions and gradually increase as you become stronger. Remember to breathe deeply and relax while doing this exercise, and maintain proper form and technique to avoid injury and achieve the best results.

Quadruped Extension-Rotation

The quadruped extension-rotation exercise is great for seniors to help relieve lower back pain and improve core strength and stability. This exercise combines extension and rotation movement, which targets the muscles in the lower back and the core.

Here's how to perform the quadruped extension-rotation exercise:

- Start on your hands and knees with your wrists directly under your shoulders and your knees directly under your hips.

- Slowly extend your right arm and left leg, keeping your hips level and stable.

- Rotate your torso to the left, reaching your right arm and left leg away from your body.

- Hold the position for a few seconds, and then return to the starting position.

- Repeat the exercise with your left arm and right leg.

- Repeat the exercise for a set number of repetitions, usually 8-12 reps and 2-3 sets for each side.

This exercise is a great way to strengthen the muscles of your lower back, core, and glutes. It's important to keep your hips level and stable while doing this exercise and to maintain proper form and technique.

It's important to start with a small number of repetitions and gradually increase as you become stronger. Remember to breathe deeply and relax while doing this exercise, and maintain proper form and technique to avoid injury and achieve the best results.

Bridging

The bridging exercise is great for seniors to help relieve lower back pain and improve core strength and stability. This exercise targets the muscles in the lower back, glutes, and core. It is a simple exercise that can be done at home and requires no equipment.

Here's how to perform the bridging exercise:

- Start by lying on your back with your knees bent and your feet flat on the floor.

- Keep your arms at your side, with your palms facing down.

- Slowly raise your hips off the floor, squeezing your glutes and lower back muscles as you do so.

- Hold the position for a few seconds, and then lower your hips back down to the starting position.

- Repeat the exercise for a set number of repetitions, usually 8-12 reps, and 2-3 sets.

This exercise works on the muscles of the lower back, glutes, and core, which are important for maintaining good posture and stability. This exercise is good for seniors as it helps to improve their flexibility and balance.

It's important to start with a small number of repetitions and gradually increase as you become stronger. Remember to breathe deeply and relax while doing this exercise, and maintain proper form and technique to avoid injury and achieve the best results.

Plank

The plank exercise is great for seniors to help relieve lower back pain and improve core strength and stability. This exercise targets the muscles in the core, including the rectus abdominis, transverse abdominis, and obliques. It is a simple exercise that can be done at home and requires no equipment.

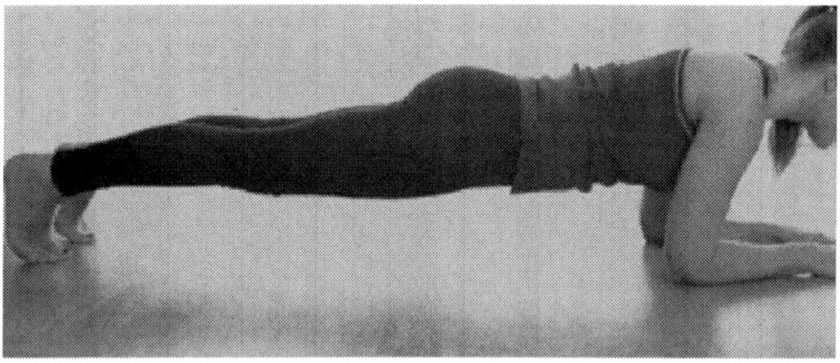

Here's how to perform the plank exercise:

- Start by lying on your stomach with your forearms on the floor and your elbows directly under your shoulders.

- Slowly raise your body off the floor, keeping your back straight and your core tight.

- Hold the position for a set amount of time, usually 20-30 seconds, and repeat 3-5 times.

Remember to breathe deeply and relax while doing this exercise, and maintain proper form and technique to avoid injury and achieve the best results.

This exercise works on the muscles of the core, which are important for maintaining good posture and stability. This exercise is also good for seniors as it helps to improve their strength, balance, and stability.

Side Plank

The side plank exercise is a variation of the plank exercise and is a great exercise for seniors to help relieve lower back pain and improve core strength and stability, as well as strengthen the muscles on the side of the body. This exercise targets the muscles in the core, including the oblique, hip, and shoulder muscles. It is a simple exercise that can be done at home and requires no equipment.

Here's how to perform the side plank exercise:

- Start by lying on your side with your elbow directly under your shoulder and your feet stacked on top of each other.

- Slowly raise your hips off the floor, keeping your body in a straight line from your head to your toes.

- Hold the position for a set amount of time, usually 20-30 seconds, and repeat 3-5 times on each side.

Remember to breathe deeply and relax while doing this exercise, and maintain proper form and technique to avoid injury and achieve the best results.

This exercise works on the muscles of the core and the side of the body, which are important for maintaining good posture and stability, as well as preventing muscle imbalances. This exercise is also good for seniors as it helps to improve their strength, balance, and stability.

It's important to start with a small amount of time and gradually increase as you become stronger.

Dead Bug

The dead bug exercise is great for seniors to help relieve lower back pain and improve core strength and stability. This exercise targets the muscles in the core, including the rectus abdominis, transverse abdominis, and obliques. It is a simple exercise that can be done at home and requires no equipment.

Here's how to perform the dead bug exercise:

- Start by lying on your back with your knees bent and your feet flat on the floor.

- Slowly lower your right arm behind your head and your left leg towards the floor, keeping your lower back pressed against the floor.

- Hold the position for a moment, and then slowly return to the starting position.

- Repeat the exercise on the other side by lowering your left arm and right leg.

- Repeat the exercise for a set number of repetitions, usually 8-12 reps, and 2-3 sets.

This exercise works on the muscles of the core which are important for maintaining good posture and stability. This exercise is also good for seniors as it helps to improve their strength and balance.

It's important to use a proper form and to start with a small number of repetitions and gradually increase as you become stronger. Remember to breathe deeply and relax while doing this exercise, and maintain proper form and technique to avoid injury and achieve the best results.

Bird Dog

The bird dog exercise is great for seniors to help relieve lower back pain and improve core strength and stability. This exercise targets the muscles in the core, including the rectus abdominis, transverse abdominis, and obliques. It's also a good exercise for balance and coordination and it can be done at home with no equipment needed.

Here's how to perform the bird-dog exercise:

- Start on your hands and knees with your wrists directly under your shoulders and your knees directly under your hips.

- Keep your core engaged and your back flat, slowly extend your right arm out in front of you and your left leg behind you.

- Keep your arms and leg in line with your body and hold the position for a moment.

- Slowly return to the starting position and repeat the exercise on the other side.

- Repeat the exercise for 8-12 reps and 2-3 sets.

This exercise is a great way to strengthen the core and improve balance and coordination. It can help seniors to improve their stability, posture, and overall well-being.

It's important to keep a proper form and to start with a small number of repetitions and gradually increase as you become stronger. Remember to breathe deeply and relax while doing this exercise, and maintain proper form and technique to avoid injury and achieve the best results.

Glute Bridge

The glute bridge exercise is a fun and effective way for seniors to relieve lower back pain and improve core strength, stability, and overall well-being. This exercise targets the muscles in the glutes, hamstrings, and core, and it's great for improving balance, coordination, and posture. Plus, it's a simple exercise that can be done at home with no equipment needed.

Here's how to perform the glute bridge exercise:

- Start by lying on your back with your knees bent and your feet flat on the floor.

- Place your arms at your sides, with your palms facing down.

- Slowly lift your hips towards the ceiling, squeezing your glutes as you do so.

- Hold the position for a moment, and then slowly lower your hips back down to the starting position.

- Repeat the exercise for 8-12 reps and 2-3 sets.

The glute bridge exercise is an effective and enjoyable way to improve your overall well-being while feeling happy and energized. It's a great way to strengthen the muscles in the core, glutes, and hamstrings and it will help you to stand taller, move more easily and look great!

It's important to use a proper form and to start with a small number of repetitions and gradually increase as you become stronger. Remember to breathe deeply and relax while doing this exercise, and maintain proper form and technique to avoid injury and achieve the best results.

It's always a good idea to consult with a healthcare professional before starting any exercise program, especially if you have a chronic condition or have had a recent injury. They can also help to adapt the exercise to your individual needs and limitations.

So, let's get moving, seniors! Let's feel strong, energized, and happy with the glute bridge exercise. It's a great way to stay active and healthy as you age. Keep smiling, keep moving, and enjoy the benefits of this fun and effective exercise!

Seated Spinal Twist

The seated spinal twist exercise is a great way for seniors to relieve lower back pain, improve flexibility, and boost overall well-being. This exercise targets the muscles in the back, core, and hips, and it's great for improving posture, balance, and coordination. Plus, it's a simple exercise that can be done at home with no equipment needed.

Here's how to perform the seated spinal twist exercise:

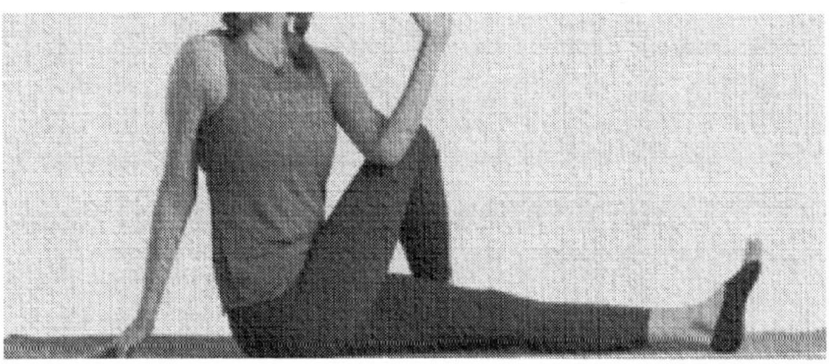

- Start by sitting on the floor with your legs extended straight out in front of you.

- Bend your right knee and place your foot on the floor next to your left knee.

- Place your left hand behind you, with your fingers pointing away from your body.

- Place your right hand on your right knee and twist your torso to the right.

- Hold the position for a moment and then release the twist and return to the starting position.

- Repeat the exercise on the other side.

- Repeat the exercise for 8-12 reps and 2-3 sets.

The seated spinal twist exercise is an effective and enjoyable way to improve your overall well-being while feeling happy and energized. It's a great way to relieve lower back pain and improve flexibility, mobility, and balance. It's also a great way to relieve stress and tension from the daily routine.

It's important to use proper form and to start with a small number of repetitions and gradually increase as you become stronger. Remember to breathe deeply and relax while doing this exercise, and maintain proper form and technique to avoid injury and achieve the best results.

So, seniors, let's get twisting! Let's feel flexible, balanced, and energized with the seated spinal twist exercise. It's a great way to stay active and healthy as you age. Keep smiling, keep moving, and enjoy the benefits of this fun and effective exercise!

Seated Forward Bend

The seated forward bend exercise is a fantastic way for seniors to relieve lower back pain, improve flexibility, and boost overall well-being. This exercise targets the muscles in the back, core, and hamstrings, and it's great for improving posture, balance, and coordination. Plus, it's a simple exercise that can be done at home with no equipment needed.

Here's how to perform the seated forward bend exercise:

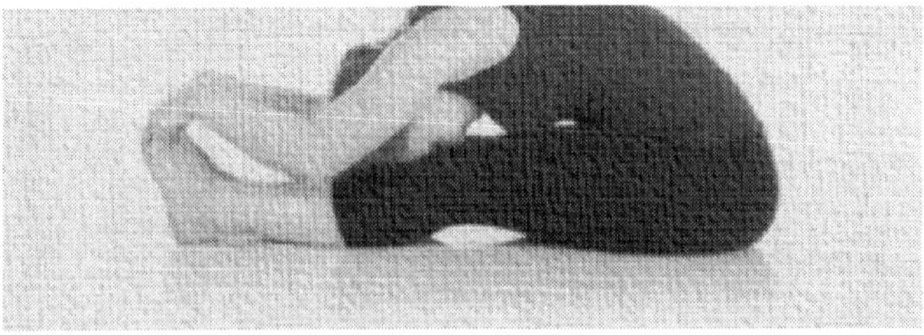

- Start by sitting on the floor with your legs extended straight out in front of you.

- Sit up tall and take a deep breath.

- Slowly begin to hinge forward from your hips, reaching towards your toes.

- Keep a slight bend in your knees if needed, and allow your head to hang heavy.

- Hold the position for a moment and then release the stretch and return to the starting position.

- Repeat the exercise for 8-12 reps and 2-3 sets.

The seated forward bend exercise is an effective and enjoyable way to improve your overall well-being while feeling happy and energized. It's a great way to relieve lower back pain, improve flexibility and boost your mood. This exercise is also a great way to relax and relieve stress from the daily routine.

It's important to use proper form and to start with a small number of repetitions and gradually increase as you become stronger. Remember to breathe deeply and relax while doing this exercise, and maintain proper form and technique to avoid injury and achieve the best results.

It's always a good idea to consult with a healthcare professional before starting any exercise program, especially if you have a chronic condition or have had a recent injury. They can also help to adapt the exercise to your individual needs and limitations.

So, seniors, let's reach for our toes! Let's feel flexible, balanced, and energized with the seated forward bend exercise. It's a great way to stay active and healthy as you age. Keep smiling, keep moving, and enjoy the benefits of this fun and effective exercise!

Seated Hamstring Stretch

The seated hamstring stretch is a fantastic exercise for seniors looking to relieve lower back pain, improve flexibility, and boost overall well-being. This exercise targets the muscles in the back of the thighs, and it's great for improving posture, balance, and coordination. Plus, it's a simple exercise that can be done at home with no equipment needed.

Here's how to perform the seated hamstring stretch:

- Start by sitting on the floor with your legs extended straight out in front of you.
- Sit up tall and take a deep breath.
- Slowly begin to reach forward, keeping your back straight, and try to touch your toes.

- Hold the stretch for 15-30 seconds, and then release the stretch and return to the starting position.

- Repeat the exercise for 8-12 reps and 2-3 sets.

The seated hamstring stretch is an effective and enjoyable way to improve your overall well-being while feeling happy and energized. It's a great way to relieve lower back pain, improve flexibility, and boost your mood. This exercise is also a great way to relax and relieve stress from the daily routine.

It's important to use proper form and to start with a small number of repetitions and gradually increase as you become stronger. Remember to breathe deeply and relax while doing this exercise, and maintain proper form and technique to avoid injury and achieve the best results.

So, seniors, let's reach for our toes! Let's feel flexible, balanced, and energized with the seated hamstring stretch exercise. It's a great way to stay active and healthy as you age. Keep smiling, keep stretching, and enjoy the benefits of this fun and effective exercise!

Seated Hip Flexor Stretch

The seated hip flexor stretch is a great exercise for seniors looking to relieve lower back pain, improve flexibility, and boost overall well-being. This exercise targets the muscles in the front of the hips, which are often tight and shortened from prolonged sitting. It's a great exercise for improving posture, balance, and coordination. Plus, it's a simple exercise that can be done at home with no equipment needed.

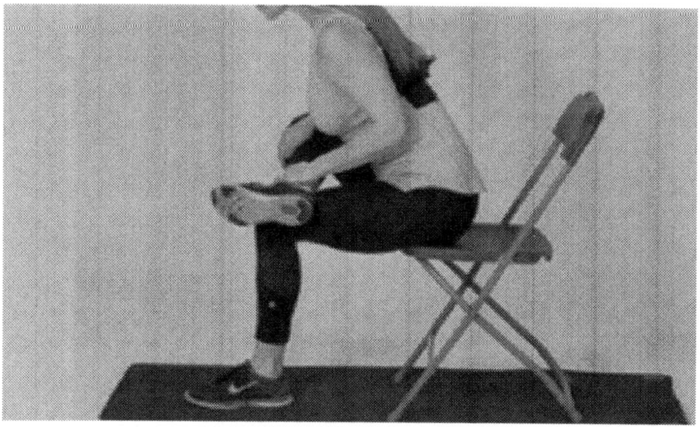

Here's how to perform the seated hip flexor stretch:

- Start by sitting on a chair, legs flat on the ground

- Sit up tall and take a deep breath.

- Slowly bring your right knee up towards your chest, keeping your back straight.

- Place your right ankle on your left knee and gently press down on your right knee with your left hand.

- Hold the stretch for 15-30 seconds, and then release the stretch and return to the starting position.

- Repeat the exercise on the other side.

- Repeat the exercise for 8-12 reps and 2-3 sets.

The seated hip flexor stretch is an effective and enjoyable way to improve your overall well-being while feeling happy and energized. It's a great way to relieve lower back pain, improve flexibility, and boost your mood. This exercise is also a great way to relax and relieve stress from the daily routine.

It's important to use proper form and to start with a small number of repetitions and gradually increase as you become stronger. Remember to breathe deeply and relax while doing this exercise, and maintain proper form and technique to avoid injury and achieve the best results.

So, seniors, let's stretch our hips! Let's feel flexible, balanced, and energized with the seated hip flexor stretch exercise. It's a great way to stay active and healthy as you age. Keep smiling, keep stretching, and enjoy the benefits of this fun and effective exercise!

Wall Slides

Wall slides are a fantastic exercise for seniors looking to relieve lower back pain, improve mobility, and build upper body strength. This exercise is easy to perform and requires no equipment, making it perfect for those who want to stay active and healthy at home.

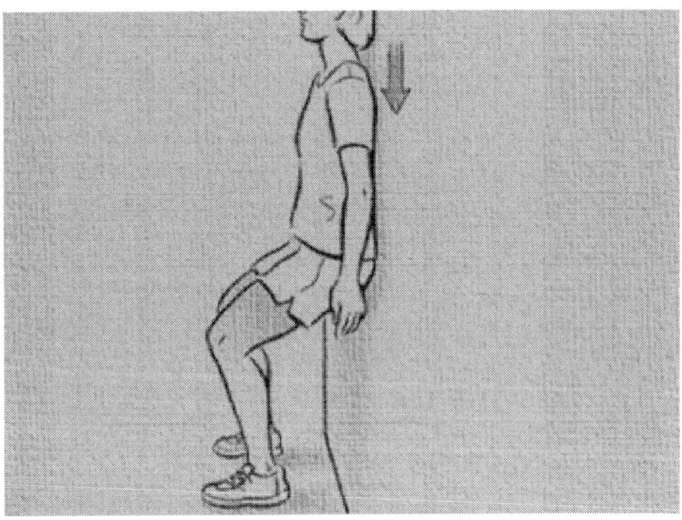

Here's how to perform a wall slide:

- Start by standing with your back against a wall and your feet shoulder-width apart.

- Slowly slide your back down the wall until you are in a seated position with your knees bent at a 90-degree angle.

- Hold this position for a few seconds and then slowly slide back up the wall to the starting position.

- Repeat this movement for 8-12 reps and 2-3 sets.

Performing wall slides is a fun and easy way to stay active, increase flexibility, and build upper body strength. This exercise can also help to improve posture and balance, which are important for maintaining independence as we age.

Wall slides are also a great way to relieve stress, and get out of the daily routine.

It's a great way to relax, breathe, and feel the benefits of exercise on your mind and body.

It's important to use proper form and to start with a small number of repetitions and gradually increase as you become stronger. Remember to breathe deeply and relax while doing this exercise, and maintain proper form and technique to avoid injury and achieve the best results.

It's always a good idea to consult with a healthcare professional before starting any exercise program, especially if you have a chronic condition or have had a recent injury. They can also help to adapt the exercise to your individual needs and limitations.

So, seniors, let's slide our way to a healthier you! Wall slides are a fun and easy way to stay active and healthy as you age. Get moving, stay strong, and enjoy the benefits of this exercise! Keep smiling, keep sliding, and enjoy the benefits of this cheerful and encouraging exercise!

Lying Leg Lifts

Lying leg lifts are a fantastic exercise for seniors looking to relieve lower back pain, improve mobility, and build lower body strength. This exercise is easy to perform and requires no equipment, making it perfect for those who want to stay active and healthy at home.

Here's how to perform a lying leg lift:

- Start by lying on your back on a mat or soft surface with your legs extended and your arms at your sides.

- Slowly raise one leg towards the ceiling, keeping the other leg extended on the ground.

- Hold this position for a few seconds and then slowly lower your leg back down to the starting position.

- Repeat this movement for 8-12 reps and 2-3 sets, then switch legs.

Performing lying leg lifts is a fun and easy way to stay active, increase flexibility, and build lower body strength. This exercise can also help to improve posture and balance, which are important for maintaining independence as we age.

Lying leg lifts are also a great way to relieve stress and get out of the daily routine. It's a great way to relax, breathe, and feel the benefits of exercise on your mind and body.

It's important to use proper form and to start with a small number of repetitions and gradually increase as you become stronger. Remember to breathe deeply and relax while doing this exercise, and maintain proper form and technique to avoid injury and achieve the best results.

It's always a good idea to consult with a healthcare professional before starting any exercise program, especially if you have a chronic condition or have had a recent injury. They can also help to adapt the exercise to your individual needs and limitations.

So, seniors, let's lift our way to a healthier you! Lying leg lifts are a fun and easy way to stay active and healthy as you age. Get moving, stay strong, and enjoy the benefits of this exercise!

Lying Hip Extensions

Lying hip extensions are a fantastic exercise for seniors looking to relieve lower back pain, improve mobility, and build strength in the hips and legs. This exercise is easy to perform and requires no equipment, making it perfect for those who want to stay active and healthy at home.

Here's how to perform a lying hip extension:

- Start by lying on your back on a mat or soft surface with your knees bent and your feet flat on the floor.

- Slowly raise one leg towards the ceiling, keeping the other foot flat on the floor.

- Hold this position for a few seconds and then slowly lower your leg back down to the starting position.

- Repeat this movement for 8-12 reps and 2-3 sets, then switch legs.

Performing lying hip extensions is a fun and easy way to stay active, increase flexibility and build strength in the hips and legs. This exercise can also help to improve posture and balance, which are important for maintaining independence as we age.

Lying hip extensions are also a great way to relieve stress and get out of the daily routine. It's a great way to relax, breathe, and feel the benefits of exercise on your mind and body.

It's important to use proper form and to start with a small number of repetitions and gradually increase as you become stronger. Remember to breathe deeply and relax while doing this exercise, and maintain proper form and technique to avoid injury and achieve the best results.

So, seniors, let's get moving and feel the burn in our hips! Lying hip extensions are a fun and easy way to stay active and healthy as you age.

Lying Knee Bends

Lying knee bends, also known as leg curls, are a fantastic exercise for seniors looking to relieve lower back pain, improve mobility, and build strength in the legs and glutes. This exercise is easy to perform and requires no equipment, making it perfect for those who want to stay active and healthy at home.

Here's how to perform a lying knee bend:

- Start by lying on your stomach on a mat or soft surface with your legs straight.

- Slowly raise one leg towards your glutes, keeping your other leg straight and your toes pointed.

- Hold this position for a few seconds and then slowly lower your leg back down to the starting position.

- Repeat this movement for 8-12 reps and 2-3 sets, then switch legs.

Performing lying knee bends is a fun and easy way to stay active, increase flexibility, and build strength in the legs and glutes. This exercise can also help to improve posture and balance, which are important for maintaining independence as we age.

Lying knee bends are also a great way to relieve stress and to get out of the daily routine. It's a great way to relax, breathe, and feel the benefits of exercise on your mind and body.

It's important to use proper form and to start with a small number of repetitions and gradually increase as you become stronger. Remember to breathe deeply and relax while doing this exercise, and maintain proper form and technique to avoid injury and achieve the best results.

So, seniors, let's get moving and feel the burn in our legs! Lying knee bends are a fun and easy way to stay active and healthy as you age.

Lying Knee Twists

Lying knee twists are a great exercise for seniors looking to relieve lower back pain, improve mobility, and build core strength. Not only is this exercise easy to perform, but it also requires no equipment, making it perfect for those who want to stay active and healthy at home.

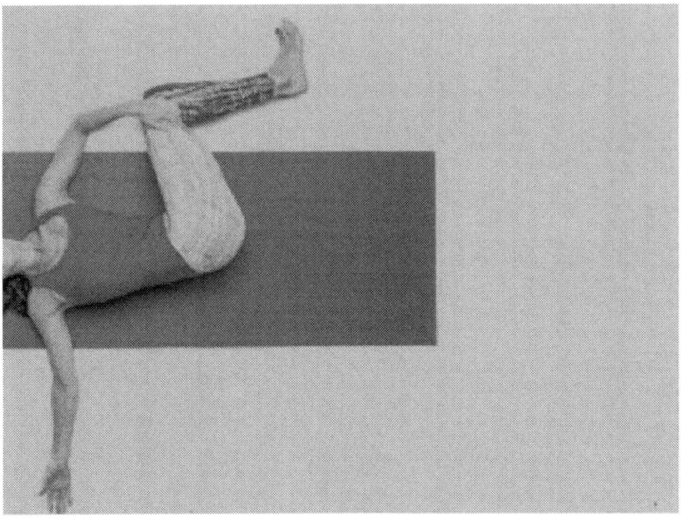

Here's how to perform a lying knee twist:

- Start by lying on your back on a mat or soft surface with your knees bent and your feet flat on the floor.

- Slowly lower both knees to one side of your body, keeping your shoulders and head on the floor.

- Hold this position for a few seconds and then slowly bring your knees back to the starting position.

- Repeat this movement for 8-12 reps and 2-3 sets, then switch sides.

Performing lying knee twists is a fun and easy way to stay active, increase flexibility, and build core strength. This exercise can also help to improve posture and balance, which are important for maintaining independence as we age.

Lying knee twists are also a great way to relieve stress and get out of the daily routine. It's a great way to relax, breathe, and feel the benefits of exercise on your mind and body.

It's important to use proper form and to start with a small number of repetitions and gradually increase as you become stronger. Remember to breathe deeply and relax while doing this exercise, and maintain proper form and technique to avoid injury and achieve the best results.

So, seniors, let's get twisting and turn up the heat on our core! Lying knee twists are a fun and easy way to stay active and healthy as you age.

Lying Hip Abductions

Lying hip abductions are a great exercise for seniors looking to relieve lower back pain, improve mobility, and build strength in the hips and legs. This exercise is easy to perform and requires no equipment, making it perfect for those who want to stay active and healthy at home.

Here's how to perform a lying hip abduction:

- Start by lying on your side on a mat or soft surface with your legs extended and your arms at your sides.

- Slowly raise the top leg towards the ceiling, keeping the bottom leg extended on the ground.

- Hold this position for a few seconds and then slowly lower your leg back down to the starting position.

- Repeat this movement for 8-12 reps and 2-3 sets, then switch sides.

- Performing lying hip abductions is a fun and easy way to stay active, increase flexibility and build strength in the hips and legs.

This exercise can also help to improve posture and balance, which are important for maintaining independence as we age.

Lying hip abductions are also a great way to relieve stress and get out of the daily routine. It's a great way to relax, breathe, and feel the benefits of exercise on your mind and body.

It's important to use proper form and to start with a small number of repetitions and gradually increase as you become stronger. Remember to breathe deeply and relax while doing this exercise, and maintain proper form and technique to avoid injury and achieve the best results.

It's always a good idea to consult with a healthcare professional before starting any exercise program, especially if you have a chronic condition or have had a recent injury. They can also help to adapt the exercise to your individual needs and limitations.

So, seniors, let's move our hips to a healthier you! Lying hip abductions are a fun and easy way to stay active and healthy as you age. Get moving, stay strong, and enjoy the benefits of this exercise!

Lying Knee Rolls

Lying knee rolls are a great exercise for seniors looking to relieve lower back pain, improve mobility and build core strength. Not only is this exercise easy to perform, but it also requires no equipment, making it perfect for those who want to stay active and healthy at home.

Here's how to perform a lying knee roll:

- Start by lying on your back on a mat or soft surface with your knees bent and your feet flat on the floor.

- Slowly lower your knees to one side of your body, keeping your shoulders and head on the floor.

- Hold this position for a few seconds and then slowly roll your knees back to the starting position.

- Repeat this movement for 8-12 reps and 2-3 sets, then switch sides.

Performing lying knee rolls is a fun and easy way to stay active, increase flexibility and build core strength. This exercise can also help to improve posture and balance, which are important for maintaining independence as we age.

Lying knee rolls are also a great way to relieve stress and get out of the daily routine. It's a great way to relax, breathe, and feel the benefits of exercise on your mind and body.

It's important to use proper form and to start with a small number of repetitions and gradually increase as you become stronger. Remember to breathe deeply and relax while doing this exercise, and maintain proper form and technique to avoid injury and achieve the best results.

So, seniors, let's roll with it! Lying knee rolls are a fun and easy way to stay active and healthy as you age.

Lying Spinal Rotations

Lying spinal rotations are a fantastic exercise for seniors looking to relieve lower back pain, improve mobility, and build core strength. This exercise is easy to perform and requires no equipment, making it perfect for those who want to stay active and healthy at home.

Here's how to perform a lying spinal rotation:

- Start by lying on your back on a mat or soft surface with your knees bent and your feet flat on the floor.

- Slowly lower your knees to one side of your body, keeping your shoulders and head on the floor.

- Hold this position for a few seconds and then slowly roll your knees back to the starting position.

- Repeat this movement for 8-12 reps and 2-3 sets, then switch sides.

Performing lying spinal rotations is a fun and easy way to stay active, increase flexibility, and build core strength. This exercise can also help to improve posture and balance, which are important for maintaining independence as we age.

Lying spinal rotations are also a great way to relieve stress and get out of the daily routine. It's a great way to relax, breathe, and feel the benefits of exercise on your mind and body.

It's important to use proper form and to start with a small number of repetitions and gradually increase as you become stronger. Remember to breathe deeply and relax while doing this exercise, and maintain proper form and technique to avoid injury and achieve the best results.

So, seniors, let's get rotating! Lying spinal rotations are a fun and easy way to stay active and healthy as you age.

Lying Spinal Extensions

Lying spinal extensions are a fantastic exercise for seniors looking to relieve lower back pain, improve mobility and build core strength. This exercise is easy to perform and requires no equipment, making it perfect for those who want to stay active and healthy at home.

Here's how to perform a lying spinal extension:

- Start by lying on your stomach on a mat or soft surface with your arms stretched out in front of you.

- Slowly lift your arms and legs off the floor, squeezing your shoulder blades together and squeezing your glutes at the same time.

- Hold this position for a few seconds and then slowly lower your arms and legs back to the starting position.

- Repeat this movement for 8-12 reps and 2-3 sets.

Performing lying spinal extensions is a fun and easy way to stay active, increase flexibility and build core strength. This exercise can also help to improve posture and balance, which are important for maintaining independence as we age.

Lying spinal extensions are also a great way to relieve stress and get out of the daily routine. It's a great way to relax, breathe, and feel the benefits of exercise on your mind and body.

It's important to use proper form and to start with a small number of repetitions and gradually increase as you become stronger. Remember to breathe deeply and relax while doing this exercise, and maintain proper form and technique to avoid injury and achieve the best results.

So, seniors, let's get extended! Lying spinal extensions are a fun and easy way to stay active and healthy as you age.

Lying Pelvic Tilts

Lying pelvic tilts are a fantastic exercise for seniors looking to relieve lower back pain, improve mobility, and strengthen the core. This exercise is easy to perform and requires no equipment, making it perfect for those who want to stay active and healthy at home.

Here's how to perform a lying pelvic tilt:

- Start by lying on your back on a mat or soft surface with your knees bent and your feet flat on the floor.

- Slowly tilt your pelvis towards your feet by tightening your abdominal muscles and pressing your lower back into the floor.

- Hold this position for a few seconds and then slowly release it, allowing your pelvis to return to a neutral position.

- Repeat this movement for 8-12 reps and 2-3 sets.

Performing lying pelvic tilts is a fun and easy way to stay active, improve flexibility, and build core strength. This exercise can also help to improve posture and balance, which are important for maintaining independence as we age.

Lying pelvic tilts are also a great way to relieve stress and get out of the daily routine. It's a great way to relax, breathe, and feel the benefits of exercise on your mind and body.

It's important to use proper form and to start with a small number of repetitions and gradually increase as you become stronger. Remember to breathe deeply and relax while doing this exercise, and maintain proper form and technique to avoid injury and achieve the best results.

So, seniors, let's get tilting! Lying pelvic tilts are a fun and easy way to stay active and healthy as you age.

Prevention and Maintenance

Importance of Proper Posture

Proper posture is important for maintaining the health of the spine and reducing the risk of lower back pain. When standing, sitting, or performing any physical activity, it's important to keep the spine in a neutral position, which means that the natural curvature of the spine is maintained.

Poor posture can cause the muscles and ligaments in the lower back to become overworked and fatigued, leading to pain and stiffness. Additionally, poor posture can also put pressure on the discs and joints in the lower back, leading to injury and degeneration over time.

Proper posture can help to distribute weight and pressure evenly throughout the body, reducing stress on the lower back. It can also help to improve breathing and circulation, and can even help to improve mood and energy levels.

Some tips for maintaining proper posture include:

- Sitting with your feet flat on the floor and your back against the chair.
- Keep your shoulders back and down and your chest lifted.
- Keeping your head and neck in line with your spine.
- Keeping your abdominal muscles tight to support your lower back.
- Sitting on an exercise ball instead of a chair engages core muscles and encourages proper posture

It's important to be mindful of your posture throughout the day and to make adjustments as needed. Regular exercise, stretching, and physical therapy can also help to improve posture and reduce the risk of lower back pain.

Lifting techniques are important for seniors to consider, as they can help to reduce the risk of injury and lower back pain. As we age, our bodies become less flexible and our muscles weaken, which can make it more difficult to lift and carry objects safely.

Here are a few tips for lifting techniques for seniors:

Use your legs: When lifting an object, it is important to use your legs and not your back. Bend your knees and keep your back straight as you lift. This will help to distribute the weight of the object evenly across your body and reduce the strain on your lower back.

Keep the object close to your body: When carrying an object, it is important to keep it as close to your body as possible. This will help to reduce the strain on your lower back and make it easier to maintain proper posture.

Avoid twisting:

Twisting your body when lifting or carrying an object can put extra strain on your lower back. Instead, face the object and turn your entire body rather than twisting your spine.

Use assistive devices:

When lifting or carrying heavy objects, consider using assistive devices such as a walker, cane, or shopping cart to help distribute the weight and reduce the strain on your lower back.

Avoid lifting heavy objects:

If an object is too heavy for you to lift safely, consider asking for help or using a dolly or hand truck to move it.

It's important to be aware of your limitations and to use proper technique when lifting and carrying objects, especially as you age to avoid injury and maintain good overall health. It is always a good idea to consult with a healthcare professional for guidance and recommendations.

Staying active and maintaining a healthy weight is important for seniors to help reduce the risk of lower back pain and other health issues. Regular physical activity and a healthy diet can help to improve overall health, increase flexibility and strength, and reduce the risk of chronic diseases.

Physical activity: Regular physical activity can help to improve flexibility, strength, and balance, which can reduce the risk of falls and lower back pain. Activities such as walking, swimming, cycling, and yoga are all great options for seniors. It is recommended that seniors engage in at least 150 minutes of moderate-intensity aerobic activity or 75 minutes of vigorous-intensity aerobic activity a week.

Maintaining a healthy weight: Being overweight or obese can put extra stress on the lower back, leading to pain and injury. Maintaining a healthy weight can help to reduce the risk of lower back pain and other health issues. A balanced diet, rich in fruits, vegetables, whole grains, lean proteins, and healthy fats, and regular physical activity can help to achieve and maintain a healthy weight.

Staying engaged: Socializing and staying engaged with others can also help to improve overall health and reduce the risk of depression, which can have a negative impact on physical and mental health. Joining clubs or groups that have similar interests, volunteering, or even taking up a new hobby can help to keep seniors active and engaged.

Conclusion

Congratulations on reaching the end of this guide on lower back pain relief exercises for seniors! By now, you should have a better understanding of the importance of exercise for relief, proper posture, and lifting techniques. You should also have a variety of exercises that you can do safely and comfortably at home to alleviate your back pain. Remember to always consult with a healthcare professional before starting any new exercise routine and to listen to your body's signals. Keep up the good work, and don't be afraid to mix and match exercises to find the best routine for you. Keep moving and stay strong!

Printed in Great Britain
by Amazon

31662201R00053